WATERS OF LIFE

an all-age
three-year
teaching and
worship
programme

intercessions

kevin
mayhew

First published in 2006 by

KEVIN MAYHEW LTD
Buxhall, Stowmarket, Suffolk, IP14 3BW
E-mail: info@kevinmayhewltd.com
Web: www.kevinmayhew.com

Intercessions is extracted from *Waters of Life – Complete
Resource book*

9 8 7 6 5 4 3 2 1 0

ISBN 1 84417 595 2
Catalogue No 1500911

Cover design by Sara-Jane Came
Compiled by Peter Dainty
Edited and typeset by Katherine Laidler

Printed in Great Britain

Contents

Introduction

This small book is a copy of the Intercessions to be used each week in the church's worship, either in the all-age part of the worship or when the younger ones have left for their own group activities. This book will help those who are going to lead the Intercessions by enabling them to look at them privately beforehand and prepare for them appropriately.

It is good to start by telling the congregation the response for the prayers and then keep a short silence before the prayers begin. Also keep a short silence after each section of prayers. The Intercessions begin with an act of praise or thanksgiving rather than plunging straight into the prayer requests. This gives people time to focus their thoughts and their attention on the ever-present God. Sometimes a piece of music playing gently in the background during the Intercessions or someone playing a single instrument can create the right feeling. A variety of people placed around the church to read different sections of the prayers can be helpful, as long as they can all be heard clearly.

DAVID ADAM

THE LORD OUR GOD
Ever-present Creator

Blessed are you Father, Son and Holy Spirit.
You have made us
and in you we live and move and have our being.
In you we rejoice.
In you is the fullness of life.

We give thanks
for the wonders and the beauty of creation.
May we delight in your world
as you delight in it.
May your Church show a great love and care for the world –
as you love and care for it.
We pray for all who do not know
of your love or your presence.
We ask you to bless all who preach the Word.

Silence

Lord of love,
in you we live and move and have our being.

We pray for all who teach us
to respect and love your world.
Bless all who work in conservation
and in protecting the resources of the earth.
Help us to enjoy the world and delight in it
with artists and musicians and all craftspeople.

Silence

Lord of love,
in you we live and move and have our being.

God, we thank you for your presence
in our homes and communities,
in our schools and in our work.
Bless our loved ones
and all who have enriched our lives by their goodness.

Silence

Lord of love,
in you we live and move and have our being.

God, we ask your presence to bring comfort and hope
to all who are struggling at this time.
We remember those injured in accidents or acts of violence,
those who are ill
and all who are in hospital.

Silence

Lord of love,
in you we live and move and have our being.

You give life and light;
in you life and light are eternal.
May all our loved ones departed and all the saints
rejoice in the fullness of eternal light and love.

Silence

Merciful Father,
**accept these prayers
for the sake of your Son,
our Saviour Jesus Christ.
Amen.**

God's Voice

Blessed are you, Lord God, Creator of all life.
We thank you because we are wonderfully made.
You have given us the gift of communication,
eyes to see, ears to hear and lips to speak.
Teach us not only to speak to you but to listen,
to be quiet in your presence
and know that you are God.

Silence

Lord, hear us:
graciously hear us.

We pray for all who listen to you in prayer
that they may speak to us of your word.
We ask your blessing upon the leaders of our churches,
upon pastors and counsellors,
upon all who are called to listen
to the needs and troubles of others.

Silence

Lord, hear us:
graciously hear us.

Guide the leaders of the nations
in the ways of justice and peace.
Keep our ears open
to the cry of the poor and the oppressed;
let us always be sensitive to the needs of others.
We pray for relief agencies
and all who are working to relieve suffering.

Silence

Lord, hear us:
graciously hear us.

Lord, in our homes help us to listen to each other
with undivided attention.
Teach us to be sensitive to the various calls for us
to share and to care for each other.
We ask you to protect our homes and loved ones.

Silence

Lord, hear us:
graciously hear us.

We remember before you all whose voices are unheard,
people who feel neglected or unwanted.
We pray for the lonely and those who have no helpers.
We remember also all who are ill at this time
at home or in hospital.

Silence

Lord, hear us:
graciously hear us.

We rejoice that you hear us and offer us eternal life.
We pray for our loved ones departed
and for all who have served you faithfully on earth.

Silence

Merciful Father,
**accept these prayers
for the sake of your Son,
our Saviour Jesus Christ.
Amen.**

Committed to God

Blessed are you, Lord our God;
in you is life and life eternal.
You love us with an everlasting love.
You give us the freedom to turn to you
or turn away from you.
You do not compel us to love you
but invite us to know you and your love.
Help us in our desire to know you
and to be more faithful to you.
Blessed are you, God, for ever.

We give you thanks for all your faithful people.
We rejoice in the fellowship of your saints
and all who have been loyal to you.
We remember before you those who are new to the faith
and all who are seeking to deepen their faith.
We pray for all who are tempted to turn their back on you,
those who are troubled by doubt
and all those who are finding their faith a challenge.

Silence

Holy Lord,
our trust is in you.

We give thanks for the gift of power you have given
to peoples and nations.
May we use all our powers to your glory
and the benefit of others.
We remember all who suffer from the misuse of power,
all who are oppressed, the wrongly imprisoned
and those who suffer from violence.
Lord, grant us peace in our hearts and in the world.

Silence

Holy Lord,
our trust is in you.

We give you thanks for those who brought us
to know you and love you.
We remember our teachers and preachers.
We pray for our friends and our families.
May our relationships all reflect
a good relationship with you.
We remember all who have been betrayed in love.

Silence

Holy Lord,
our trust is in you.

We give thanks for all who have committed themselves
to work for your glory and the benefits of others.
We remember all who feel let down, deserted or lonely.
We pray for the persecuted and the marginalised in society.
We ask your blessing on all who are ill at home
or in hospital,
on all who seek healing or deliverance.

Silence

Holy Lord,

our trust is in you.
You, Lord, are the giver of life eternal.
We remember before you the faithful departed.
We ask your blessing upon loved ones and friends
who are at rest with you.
May they rejoice in the fellowship of the saints
and the fullness of life eternal.

Silence

Merciful Father,
**accept these prayers
for the sake of your Son,
our Saviour Jesus Christ.
Amen.**

God's Growing Kingdom

Blessed are you, Lord God.
You give the increase to our sowing,
to our work and to our plantings.
You are the giver of life and life in abundance.
May we put our faith in your goodness
and, when we have sown, trust the increase to you.
Though our faith is often small, it is in a Mighty God.
Blessed are you, Father, Son and Holy Spirit.

We give thanks for those who taught us the faith,
who sowed the seed of the Gospel in our hearts.
We ask your blessing upon preachers and teachers,
upon ministers of the word and the sacraments.
We remember homes where the word of God is sown
and children are given the chance
to grow in the kingdom.
We pray for the Bible Society,
for all who produce and translate the Bible.

Silence

Lord our God,
your kingdom come in us as it is in heaven.

Lord, we long for the time
when the kingdoms of the world
will become the kingdom of Christ our Lord.
May the rulers on earth reflect the gentle and loving rule
of your kingdom in heaven.
We pray for all who are striving to do your will
in their places of work and in their homes,
for all who witness to you by their way of life.

Silence

Lord our God,
your kingdom come in us as it is in heaven.

We give thanks for those who love us
and show us through their lives

a glimpse of your kingdom.
We ask your blessing upon our homes
and our loved ones.
We remember all who suffer from violence or neglect
in their homes,
all who feel uncared for or unwanted.
We pray for the lonely
and those who have been taken into care.

Silence

Lord our God,
your kingdom come in us as it is in heaven.

We give thanks for the work of healing in our hospitals
and through the healing professions.
We pray for our own doctor.
We remember areas of the world where there is little care
or where the problems seem to overwhelm
those who seek to help.
We remember peoples caught up in disasters,
in floods, in drought or in war.
We pray for relief agencies and all who contribute to them.

Silence

Lord our God,
your kingdom come in us as it is in heaven.

We give thanks for all the saints,
for those who spread the word of God,
for those who witnessed to your love,
for those who brought the Gospel to this land.
We remember all our loved ones who are departed from us
and pray that they may rejoice
in the fullness of your kingdom.

Silence

Merciful Father,
**accept these prayers
for the sake of your Son,
our Saviour Jesus Christ.
Amen.**

God with Us

Blessed are you, Lord our God.
You never leave us or forsake us.
You have promised us the victory
through our Lord Jesus Christ.
Lord, help us to know you and to trust in you always.
Let us know that in you is the gift of life eternal
and that through you we have the power
to survive whatever happens to us or to the world.
Blessed are you, God Almighty,
Father, Son and Holy Spirit.

We give thanks for those who have taught us the faith
and brought us to know you, O God.
We ask your blessing on preachers
and teachers of the Word,
upon theological colleges and their students.
We remember any who are struggling with their faith
at this time,
all who are tempted to despair and to give up.
We pray especially for all who are sorely troubled
by circumstances or relationships.

Silence

Lord, in our darkness,
let your light shine.

As we give thanks for the world and its beauty,
we remember before you all areas of conflict and disaster.
We ask your blessing upon all who are suffering
from natural disasters such as flood or famine,
all who are driven off their land by war or tyranny.
We pray for all who are denied minimum rights and wages
and those who live as slaves.
We ask your blessing on all who work
for the good of the world and humankind.

Silence

Lord, in our darkness,
let your light shine.

We give thanks for our homes and our loved ones.
We pray for all families who are suffering
from a breakdown in relationships,
where there is tension and discord,
where there is violence or neglect.
We ask your blessing upon all who are seeking
to improve the neighbourhood in which they live.
We pray for counsellors and carers.

Silence

Lord, in our darkness,
let your light shine.

We rejoice in your love and care for us at all times.
We remember before you
all who have faced trouble or disaster this week.
We ask your blessing upon those who are ill
and whose illness finds no cure;
on all who have been injured in accidents
or who have suffered at the hands of others.
We pray especially for those whose future looks bleak
and who live in fear.

Silence

Lord, in our darkness,
let your light shine.

We give thanks for your everlasting love.
We rejoice in the saints who have witnessed to you
and to their faith in life eternal.
We remember friends and loved ones
who have departed from us
and pray that they may rejoice
in the fullness of your love
and their presence in your kingdom.

Silence

Merciful Father,
**accept these prayers
for the sake of your Son,
our Saviour Jesus Christ.
Amen.**

Loving God

Blessed are you, Father, Son and Holy Spirit,
the one and only God:
to you be praise and glory for ever.
We love you, O God, with all our heart, with all our soul,
with all our mind and with all our strength.
We come to give ourselves to you
as you give yourself to us.
Blessed be God for ever.

Father, we give thanks for all who have loved you deeply
and revealed your love to us.
We pray for all who teach from the Scriptures
and for all who preach.
We remember the young in the faith
and pray for their enthusiasm.
We remember also all who have served you
for a long time;
may they still have warm hearts and a living faith.
We ask you to bless all who minister in your name.
May the Church reveal your love and your glory
in the world.
We pray for all who seek to dedicate themselves to you
through baptism, confirmation and ordination.

Silence

God of love and mercy,
hear us as we call to you.

We give thanks for all who have used their minds
to improve and care for our world.
We ask you to guide the work of scientists,
inventors and explorers.
We pray for all who seek to expand our knowledge
and who work on the boundaries of science.
We ask you to give wisdom to all who deal with
genetic engineering in humans and in plants.
We pray for musicians and artists,
for craftspeople and all who enrich our world.

Silence

God of love and mercy,
hear us as we call to you.

We give thanks for our homes
and all places where we have learnt of love.
We ask your blessing upon our families and friends.
We pray for all who feel unloved and unwanted,
for the neglected
and all who suffer from violence or cruelty.

Silence

God of love and mercy,
hear us as we call to you.

We give thanks for our talents and abilities
and we remember before you
all whose powers are waning
or who feel that they cannot cope with life.
We pray for all who are weakened
by illness or circumstance,
all who are deeply in debt.
We ask your blessing upon those who feel unfulfilled
or thwarted in leading a meaningful and joyful life.

Silence

God of love and mercy,
hear us as we call to you.

We give thanks that you love us with an everlasting love.
When we forget you, you do not forget us.
We rejoice in the promise of life eternal
and remember in your presence
the saints who gave themselves fully to you.
We pray for all our loved ones who are departed from us.

Silence

Merciful Father,
accept these prayers
for the sake of your Son,
our Saviour Jesus Christ.
Amen.

GOD FEEDS US
The Bread of Life

Blessed are you, Father, Son and Holy Spirit.
You have created us out of your love and for your love.
You have made our hearts to long for you
and nothing else will fully satisfy them.
Help us to turn to you in our hunger and thirst,
that in you and your love
we may find refreshment and life.
You, Lord, are the giver of life in all its fullness.
Blessed are you, God, for ever.

We give thanks for all who sustain us in life
with their love and care.
Bless those who seek to bring us to the Bread of Life
and all who seek to help to provide us
with our spiritual needs.
We pray for all who celebrate the sacraments
and for those being prepared
to make their first Communion.
We remember in your presence all who are pilgrims
and seekers,
those who long for your love and wish to serve you.
We ask you to guide any who feel they have lost their way
and put too much trust in material things alone.

Silence

Lord, you alone
are our strength and hope.

We give you thanks for all who work to provide us
with food and refreshment.
We remember those who provide us with bread:
the farmers, the millers, the bakers and the shops.
We ask you to guide all who are caught up
in materialism and consumerism.

We remember especially all who have lost sight
of the deeper meaning of life.
We pray for all who are unemployed
and those who suffer from hunger or homelessness,
all who lack the necessary resources for their well-being.

Silence

Lord, you alone
are our strength and hope.

Lord, we give thanks for our homes
and for all who care for us.
We pray for our friends and our loved ones.
We remember our community:
its schools and its places of work.
May all reflect your glory and your love.
Let us be aware of any who are lonely or feel rejected.

Silence

Lord, you alone
are our strength and hope.

We give thanks for the renewing powers of our bodies
and for all who share in the healing and care of others.
We pray for all who feel their lives are empty
or meaningless,
all who feel they have wasted their lives
or never fully lived.
We remember also friends and loved ones who are ill.

Silence

Lord, you alone
are our strength and hope.

Lord, we put our trust in you.
We believe that in you is the gift of eternal life.
We pray that through you and your love
we may be brought at the last
to the fullness of your kingdom.

We remember in your presence the Blessed Virgin Mary
and all the saints departed.
We ask you to bless all our loved ones
whom we see no longer.

Silence

Merciful Father,
**accept these prayers
for the sake of your Son,
our Saviour Jesus Christ.
Amen.**

Bread from Heaven

Blessed are you, Lord our God,
for you provided for your children.
In the wilderness of this world
you give us the bread of life.
Lord, grant, as we journey towards the Promised Land,
that we may put our hope and our trust in you.
Blessed are you, Father, Son and Holy Spirit.

Father, we give you thanks that you have called us
to know you and to love you.
You have drawn us to you with bands of love.
Help us to listen and to obey your word.
We pray for all preachers and pastors,
for ministers of the word and of the sacraments.
We remember before you all who do not know or love you
and we ask your blessing upon all
who reach out in mission and love to them.
We pray for any who have lost faith in themselves
or in you.

Silence

Lord our God,
our hope is in you.

Lord God, Creator of heaven and earth,
we pray for the nations of the world.
May they find a unity and a peace in you.
We ask your blessing upon the work of the United Nations
and upon all peacekeeping forces.
We pray for areas of the world
where there is strife and division,
where people are unable to trust each other,
where people do not listen to each other.
We remember displaced peoples and refugees.

Silence

Lord our God,
our hope is in you.

We thank your for the love and protection of our homes.
We ask your blessing upon our families and friends.
We remember before you
homes where there is division or distrust,
where families are divided.
We pray for all who have been betrayed or deserted.
We remember also all who are leaving home
for the first time.

Silence

Lord our God,
our hope is in you.

We give you thanks for our own well-being
and for all that feeds our bodies, minds and spirits.
We remember all who are struggling
with doubt, depression and despair,
all who are having difficulty in their daily lives.
We pray for all who are ill at home or in hospital,
especially those who have no one
to care for them or visit them.

Silence

Lord our God,
our hope is in you.

We rejoice that you sustain us with the Bread of Life.
Through our union with Jesus you offer us life eternal.
As we celebrate our communion with the saints,
we remember our friends and loved ones departed
and ask that they may rejoice
in the fullness of eternal life.

Silence

Merciful Father,
accept these prayers
for the sake of your Son,
our Saviour Jesus Christ.
Amen.

Jesus Feeds 5000

Blessed are you, Lord our God,
in your love and care for your creation.
You do not turn away any who come to you.
You come to meet the seekers
and provide refreshment for all who hunger and thirst.
You care for the broken and the fragmented
and want nothing to be lost.
Blessed are you, Father, Son and Holy Spirit.

We come to you, dear Lord, as seekers;
we are hungry for your love and your care.
We ask you to bless all who are pilgrims and seekers,
all who long for an awareness
of your presence and your power.
We remember before you
all who bring healing and refreshment to your people.
We pray for preachers and pastors,
for leaders of prayer groups and retreat conductors
and for all places of pilgrimage.

Silence

Lord, have mercy:
let us know your compassion and care.

We give thanks for our daily bread
and for all who provide us with our food and shelter.
We pray for farmers and fishermen,
for those who work in our shops
and all who prepare food for us to eat.
We remember before you all who are hungry and weary.
We ask you to bless all who suffer
from poverty, from famine or from natural disasters.
We pray especially for the world poor
and those who are deeply in debt.

Silence

Lord, have mercy:
let us know your compassion and care.

We give you thanks for the comfort and security
of our homes.
Lord, give your blessing to all our loved ones
and friends.
We pray for any who may feel lonely or uncared for
within our community.
We remember all carers, social workers and helpers.

Silence

Lord, have mercy:
let us know your compassion and care.

Lord, we bring before you all whose lives are fragmented;
people who are broken in body, mind or spirit.
We remember all who feel shattered and exhausted,
all who long for your healing touch.
We pray for all who seek hope and peace,
that they may come to you and rest in your presence.

Silence

Lord, have mercy:
let us know your compassion and care.

You are the God who takes our weakness
and makes us strong.
We come to you as mortals
and you offer us immortality.
In your loving presence,
we remember friends and loved ones departed
and ask that not one is lost
but gathered into the fullness of joy in your kingdom.

Silence

Merciful Father,
accept these prayers
for the sake of your Son,
our Saviour Jesus Christ.
Amen.

Holy Communion

Blessed are you, Lord our God,
you give us life and love.
We rejoice in your presence that is ever with us.
We give thanks for the offering of Jesus on the cross
and for the memorial we have this Eucharist.
May we remember that he comes to us
and asks us to offer ourselves to him.
Blessed are you, Father, Son and Holy Spirit.

Father, we thank you for the revealing of your Son
in the breaking of the bread and in the taking of the wine.
We pray for all who celebrate the memorial
of the death and passion of Jesus.
We ask you to bless all who strive
for unity and fellowship within the whole Church.
May we show that we are Christians
by our love and our sharing.

Silence

Lord, may we abide in you
and know you are with us.

We give thanks for the fruits of the earth
and for all that you have given us.
As we give thanks for our daily bread
we remember all who are celebrating
growth and increase in their lives.
We pray for those in new work
or preparing to go to new schools.
We ask you to bless all artists and craftspeople,
all who enrich our world with their talents and goodness.
We remember all who provide us with food
and our daily needs.

Silence

Lord, may we abide in you
and know you are with us.

We give you thanks and praise for our homes,
for their peace and protection.
We ask your blessing on all homes
where there is disunity or discord.
We pray for all who are suffering
from a breakdown in relationships.
We pray for homes where there is a new birth
or someone newly admitted into their family.

Silence

Lord, may we abide in you
and know you are with us.

We give thanks that Jesus has shared our grief and sorrows.
As we give thanks for the wine of communion,
we remember all whose lives are being out-poured.
We pray for all who are facing pain or weakness,
all who feel diminished by the trials of life.
We remember those whose energies are failing
and any who are finding it hard to cope with life.

Silence

Lord, may we abide in you
and know you are with us.

We celebrate our Communion with you, O God,
and with the whole Church on earth and in heaven.
We rejoice in the resurrection of our Lord.
We pray for all our loved ones departed from us:
may they, with all the saints,
enjoy the fullness of your presence and your kingdom.

Silence

Merciful Father,
accept these prayers
for the sake of your Son,
our Saviour Jesus Christ.
Amen.

GOOD PEOPLE
Saints

Blessed are you, Lord our God,
for you have called us out of darkness
into your own most marvellous light.
You call us to know and to love you.
Grant that our lives may help to reveal
your love and glory in the world.
As you have called each of us to be saints
may we be worthy of our calling.
Blessed be Father, Son and Holy Spirit.

O Lord God, we rejoice in the fellowship of all your saints
and we give thanks for all who have enriched
our world and our lives by their examples.
We thank you for (N), our patron saint
and for this church in his/her name.
Bless all who are striving to live godly and holy lives.
We remember in your presence
all who are growing in the faith,
those in Sunday schools, study groups
and confirmation classes.
We pray for all who feel called to be priests, deacons
or teachers of the faith.
Lord, we ask your blessing on our lives
that we may be the people you want us to be
and do what you want us to do.

Silence

Lord, make us to be numbered with your saints
in glory everlasting.

We give thanks for all who have served the world
in their vocation.
We pray for kings and queens, princes and rulers.

We remember Elizabeth our queen.
We ask your blessing and guidance
on all who hold positions of authority
or who influence the lives of others.
We pray for all who quietly give themselves
in the service of the community in which they live.
Bless all who are carers
and those who are an example for us to follow.

Silence

Lord, make us to be numbered with your saints
in glory everlasting.

As we give thanks for our homes and loved ones,
make us aware of the quiet sacrifice and love
that is often given unheeded.
We thank you for all that our parents have done for us
and for any who have been benefactors in our lives.
We ask your blessing upon all who suffer
from violence or neglect in their homes,
all who are discouraged and disheartened
by their surroundings
and any who lack a good example to follow.

Silence

Lord, make us to be numbered with your saints
in glory everlasting.

We give thanks
for the saints who have triumphed through suffering
and have revealed your glory
despite persecution and pain.
We ask your blessing upon all who are struggling
at this time.
We remember those caught up in vice, drugs or crime
and who cannot find a way out.
We pray for victims of terrorism or war,
remembering stateless and homeless people.
We bring before you friends and loved ones who are ill
and all who fear the future.

Silence

Lord, make us to be numbered with your saints
in glory everlasting.

We give thanks for all who have served you on earth
and now are at rest in your kingdom.
We pray for friends and loved ones
who are departed from us,
asking that as they shared their love with us on earth
they may know your love in eternal life.
We rejoice in the fellowship of all your saints
and pray that we may share with them
in your eternal kingdom.

Silence

Merciful Father,
accept these prayers
for the sake of your Son,
our Saviour Jesus Christ.
Amen.

Service and Suffering

Blessed are you, Lord our God.
You give us the opportunity to meet you
in the call of the poor and in the cries of the needy.
Give us the courage to serve
and to share in the love that you have for all people.
Teach us to be attentive and open to others
for in meeting them we meet you.
Blessed are you, Father, Son and Holy Spirit.

Father, we give you thanks for all who have cared for us
and brought us to know you and your love.
We ask your blessing on all who serve
as ministers and priests within your church.
May our churches be ready
to serve the needs of our community and the world.
We remember all who give their lives
to relieve the sorrows and suffering of their fellow beings.

Silence

Lord, as we draw near to you,
help us to know you are ever with us.

As we rejoice in your goodness and grace,
we remember all who hunger, all who are homeless,
all refugees and stateless peoples.
We remember ethnic minorities
who are suffering from persecution.
We pray for those who suffer through war and violence.
We ask your blessing on all who are underpaid
and treated as slaves
to provide richer people with cheap goods.
We pray for all Fair Trade organisations.

Silence

Lord, as we draw near to you,
help us to know you are ever with us.

We give thanks to you for the love and care
we have in our homes.

We remember how much we are served
and looked after by our parents.
May we never take them or any who care for us
for granted.
May we learn to help as much as we can
within our own homes.
We ask you to bless all homes
where there is poverty or great debt.
We remember also homes where some individuals
are ignored or taken for granted.

Silence

Lord, as we draw near to you,
help us to know you are ever with us.

Lord, we pray for areas of poverty and bad housing
throughout our world.
We remember all who do not have the basic needs
of care and attention.
We ask your blessing upon all who are ill
and those who feel lonely or neglected.
We remember especially children separated
from their loved ones
and children taken into care.

Silence

Lord, as we draw near to you,
help us to know you are ever with us.

Teach us, good Lord, to serve you as you deserve:
to give and not to count the cost.
Grant that we may learn to be generous and gracious
as are your saints who now rejoice in your kingdom.
We rejoice in the fellowship of all your saints
and ask your blessing
upon our loved ones who are departed from us.

Silence

Merciful Father,
**accept these prayers
for the sake of your Son,
our Saviour Jesus Christ.
Amen.**

Good Inside and Out

Blessed are you, Lord our God.
You give us life, you give us love, you give us yourself.
We come to give our lives and our love to you.
Cleanse us from all our sin
and make a clean heart within us,
that we may do what you want us to do
and be the people you want us to be.

We give thanks for the examples of the saints
in their battle against evil and in their striving to do good.
We remember before you
all who are struggling with temptation,
all who are pulled by divided loyalties.
We pray for those who go through the rituals
but miss the reality.
We ask your blessing
on all who are scorned, rejected or persecuted.
because of their relationship with Christ.

Silence

Make our hearts clean, O God;
renew a right spirit within us.

We give thanks for the work of the Social Services
and all who work for the care of others.
We remember before you
all who are caught up in vice or degradation.
We pray for all addicts,
that they may find help and hope.
Bless all who struggle to keep standards
and make a stand against the evils that are around them.

Silence

Make our hearts clean, O God;
renew a right spirit within us.

We rejoice in our homes and in family life.
We thank you for all who have given their lives
in caring for us and in loving us.
We ask your blessing upon our families and friends.
We remember before you all who are lonely,
all who feel uncared for or unwanted.
We pray for all who suffer from neglect
or a breakdown in relationships.

Silence

Make our hearts clean, O God;
renew a right spirit within us.

As we rejoice in life, we remember all who feel
that life is meaningless and empty.
We ask your blessing on the despairing and despondent.
We pray for all who are treated as unclean
through illness or disability.
We remember all who work to combat disease
and infections.

Silence

Make our hearts clean, O God;
renew a right spirit within us.

We rejoice in the fellowship of all your saints.
We remember before you all our loved ones departed,
giving thanks for their life and their care.
We offer our hearts and minds and whole being to you,
good and gracious God.

Silence

Merciful Father,
**accept these prayers
for the sake of your Son,
our Saviour Jesus Christ.
Amen.**

ADVENT
Waiting for God

As we begin another Church Year
let us give thanks to God that he has made us,
that he loves us
and that he comes to us.

O God, you are our Maker:
you give us life, you give us love,
your give us yourself.
Help us to give our lives, our love
and ourselves to you.
Keep us alert and aware of your presence,
that we may meet you each day
and know that you come to us in grace and in love.

Lord, as you come to your Church,
help us to reveal your glory.
Grant that we may show your grace
and your goodness in our lives.
We thank you for the grace and goodness
revealed in Jesus Christ
and that we are enriched in him.

We remember churches that are struggling
against the darkness of evil, of opposition, of apathy.
We remember especially
Christians who are being persecuted for their faith.

Silence

Come, Lord Jesus;
come, our Saviour and our God.

As we pray for your world,
we remember those who are seeking
to bring peace and goodwill among all.
We pray for those involved in war or the threat of war.
We think of those caught up in earthquakes,
famine or flood.

Silence

Come, Lord Jesus;
come, our Saviour and our God.

Lord, let your presence be known
in our homes and our actions.
May people be thankful for us
and our care of all that is around us.
We pray that you will show yourself to us
through our loved ones and friends.

Silence

Come, Lord Jesus;
come, our Saviour and our God.

We remember all whose lives are darkened
by pain and distress;
all who are struggling with doubt and despair;
all whose faith is shaken
by what is happening around them.
We pray for members of our community and friends
who are ill at this time.

Silence

Come, Lord Jesus;
come, our Saviour and our God.

God our Father, your grace has been given to us,
in the gift of eternal life and in your abiding presence.
We pray for all who are departed from us,
for friends and loved ones
in the fullness of your eternal kingdom.
We rejoice with them in the gift of life and your love.

Silence

Merciful Father,
accept these prayers
for the sake of your Son,
our Saviour Jesus Christ.
Amen.

Prepared?

We pray that we and your whole Church
may be prepared for your coming to us.
When you come
may you find us a holy and a godly people;
may you find us striving for peace
and looking forward to your glory.

Silence

Lord, change us:
and we shall be changed.

We remember today all who are being baptised.
We pray for the parents and the godparents.
We come with all who are sorry for their sins
and want to lead a new life;
with all who seek forgiveness and cleansing.

Silence

Lord, change us:
and we shall be changed.

We remember all who are striving for peace.
Bless the leaders of nations and peacekeeping forces.
Guide the United Nations and the work of relief agencies.
May we strive for justice and freedom for all peoples.

Silence

Lord, change us:
and we shall be changed.

Lord, we ask that our homes
may be places of welcome, love and harmony.
May we make room for you in our lives and our work.

Silence

Lord, change us:
and we shall be changed.

We come before you with all who are struggling:
those who are ill at home or in hospital;
the world poor, the oppressed
and all who suffer from violence or rejection.
We ask that we may know your healing presence.

Silence

Lord, change us:
and we shall be changed.

And we remember before you all who have died,
our friends and loved ones departed
and all your saints.

Silence

Merciful Father,
accept these prayers
for the sake of your Son,
our Saviour Jesus Christ.
Amen.

The Messiah

Eternal light shine in our hearts,
that our days may be bright with your presence.
May we be aware
of the great things that you have done for us
and rejoice in your salvation.

We remember all who walk in darkness
and do not know the love of God.
We remember those who have never heard the Good News.
We pray that the whole Church may reach out
in mission, in service and in love.
We pray especially for the Church
where it has lost vision or sense of outreach.

Silence

Eternal light,
shine in our hearts.

Remember our world where people are oppressed;
where there is hunger and poverty.
We ask you to strengthen all who work for peace
and to relieve the poor.
At this time we pray especially for . . .
May we do all that we can to help.

Silence

Eternal light,
shine in our hearts.

We give you thanks for our homes and our loved ones,
for the freedom and the peace that is ours.
May we be sensitive to the needs of those around us
and be of help when we can.

Silence

Eternal light,
shine in our hearts.

God give strength and courage to all who are ill,
to those involved in accidents or acts of violence.
We remember those who have lost their freedom
or their homes.
We pray especially for . . .
We give thanks for all who work in hospitals
and for our own doctors.

Silence

Eternal light,
shine in our hearts.

We rejoice that you have freed us
from the slavery of sin and death
and brought us to the glorious liberty
of the children of God.
We rejoice in the gift of eternal life,
and pray for friends and loved ones departed.

Silence

Merciful Father,
**accept these prayers
for the sake of your Son,
our Saviour Jesus Christ.
Amen.**

Welcome?

O God, as we prepare for Christmas
may we be ready for your coming to us.
As we make space for friends and relatives
may we make room in our lives for you.
In our daily living let us seek to do your will
and help to bring in your kingdom.

Through the working of the Church,
through obedience to you,
through reaching out in mission,
through the proclaiming of the Gospel,
your kingdom come:
your will be done.

Through our striving for peace,
through our caring for the poor,
through our desire for justice,
through the ways we seek to improve your world,
your kingdom come:
your will be done.

Through our love in our homes,
through our honesty and sensitivity,
through our relationships and friends,
through our hopes and our ambitions,
your kingdom come:
your will be done.

Through the healing of the ill,
through looking after the lonely,
through our compassion and care,
your kingdom come:
your will be done.

We remember especially today
any who have asked for our prayers
or who are in trouble or danger.

We ask that we may share with them
in the fullness of your kingdom.

Silence

Merciful Father,
**accept these prayers
for the sake of your Son,
our Saviour Jesus Christ.
Amen.**

CHRISTMAS
Shepherds and Angels

Lord God, we thank you for the gift of sight
and for the deeper sight
that lets us see you at work in your world.
We pray that our vision may not be impaired
but that we may see you more clearly
and love you more dearly day by day.

We give thanks for the Church throughout the world
and the telling of the Good News.
We pray for all evangelists and preachers,
for pastors and ministers,
for all who have the care of your people.
Teach us to ponder on their words
and treasure them in our hearts.

Silence

May we see you more clearly
and love you more dearly.

We remember all who work to provide us
with food and shelter.
We pray for shepherds and farmers,
for all food producers.
We remember all who work in shops and factories.

Silence

May we see you more clearly
and love you more dearly.

We thank you for our homes and our loved ones.
We remember those who taught us the faith.
We pray for our teachers
and all who have been an example to us.

Silence

May we see you more clearly
and love you more dearly.

We remember today all whose sight is impaired.
We pray for all who have lost vision
or hope in the world,
all who feel lonely,
all who have lost a sense of wonder.
We pray especially for those who are ill
at home or in hospital.

Silence

May we see you more clearly
And love you more dearly.

We ask that we may have a vision of your presence
and of your eternal kingdom.
We pray for our loved ones
who have passed from our sight.

Silence

Merciful Father,
**accept these prayers
for the sake of your Son,
our Saviour Jesus Christ.
Amen.**

EPIPHANY
Christ for all Peoples

God, we give thanks to you
for your love towards all peoples of the world.
You have chosen to give yourself to us all
and invite us to give ourselves to you.
Blessed are you, Lord God, for all things come from you
and of your own do we give you.
We come in our poverty to your riches,
in our foolishness to your wisdom,
in our sorrows to your healing and joy.

Silence

Light of Christ,
shine in our lives.

As we remember the wise men,
we pray for the rich and the comfortable,
all who have plenty of this world's good things.
May they know that all things come from you
and their lives are a gift from you.
May the riches of the world be put to good use.
We remember the world's poor,
the homeless and the hungry.

Silence

Light of Christ,
shine in our lives.

We pray for all who are seekers,
who search for the truth,
who look for meaning
and who desire to know you.
We pray for pilgrim peoples,
especially those on their way to Bethlehem
or Jerusalem.

We pray for those who are new to our church
or community.

Silence

Light of Christ,
shine in our lives.

We give thanks for all who come to you in worship,
all who are aware of awe or mystery in their lives.
We pray for leaders of worship, choirs and organists,
for all who give us a sense of wonder and beauty.

Silence

Light of Christ,
shine in our lives.

We come with all who are in pain or sorrow.
We remember those whose sickness finds no cure,
those who are permanently ill
and those with a short time to live.
We pray for doctors and nurses
and all who are involved in healing.

Silence

Light of Christ,
shine in our lives.

Lord, we worship and adore you.
We offer you our joys and sorrows,
our sickness and health,
our riches and our poverty.
We remember all who have enriched our lives
by their goodness.
We pray for loved ones who are now in the fullness
of your kingdom.

Silence

Merciful Father,
**accept these prayers
for the sake of your Son,
our Saviour Jesus Christ.
Amen.**

JESUS
Baptism

We rejoice in your presence and your love,
Father, Son and Holy Spirit.
You have made us, you have redeemed us,
and you guide us.
We remember in your presence
all who are being prepared for baptism or confirmation:
all who are seeking to know the gifts of the Spirit.
We pray for our own clergy
and for all who are being prepared
for ordination and ministry.

Silence

God ever with us:
hear us, Father, Son and Holy Spirit.

We pray for all who are starting new work or new studies,
for the newly married and the newly engaged,
for all who are testing their vocations.
We pray for all who seek to bring peace to our world.

Silence

God ever with us:
hear us, Father, Son and Holy Spirit.

We give thanks for our homes and our loved ones,
for our godparents and our godchildren.
We ask your blessing upon them.
We remember all who come from broken homes
or who are suffering from broken relationships.

Silence

God ever with us:
hear us, Father, Son and Holy Spirit.

We pray for all who feel they have lost their way,
who are troubled and distressed,
that they may know your love and care.
We remember also those who are ill at home or in hospital,
all who are struggling at this time.

Silence

God ever with us:
hear us, Father, Son and Holy Spirit.

We praise you for giving us life and life eternal.
We remember especially today
friends and loved ones who have enriched our lives
but who are now departed from this world.
We commend all to you, Father, Son and Holy Spirit.

Silence

Merciful Father,
accept these prayers
for the sake of your Son,
our Saviour Jesus Christ.
Amen.

At a Wedding

You, O Lord, are almighty, endless in power and in love.
When we have no power to help ourselves
help us to know we can trust in you,
in your presence and in your power.

We pray for the Church
that it may know its true resources and power
are from you;
that it may be enabled
to proclaim your saving power and your love.
Give your Church the ability
to be a healing instrument in the world,
to bring peace,
and to proclaim your presence.

Silence

Almighty God,
we know all power comes from you.

We remember all who struggle for survival,
the poor and the oppressed,
the hungry and the homeless,
all who feel powerless.
We ask you to bless all
who strive to bring justice and peace to our world.

Silence

Almighty God,
we know all power comes from you.

We give thanks for all who have enriched our lives
by their love and goodness.
We ask that your love may be experienced in our homes
and among our loved ones and friends.

We pray for homes where there is conflict,
violence or abuse,
especially for any who live in fear
or feel unable to change.

Silence

Almighty God,
we know all power comes from you.

Give strength to the weak,
refresh the weary,
encourage the fearful
and protect all who are endangered.
We remember friends and loved ones
who are ill or in need of comfort and refreshment.

Silence

Almighty God,
we know all power comes from you.

We rejoice that you give us life in all its abundance
and life eternal.
We pray for all our loved ones departed
that they may have the fullness of life in your kingdom.

Silence

Merciful Father,
**accept these prayers
for the sake of your Son,
our Saviour Jesus Christ.
Amen.**

Sent with God's Love

Blessed are you, Lord, God of all creation.
The whole universe belongs to you
and yet you care for each one of us.
You come to us in love to be our Saviour and our friend.
You have chosen us to be your people
and given us of your Holy Spirit
We give you thanks and praise.

We share with all who continue to give thanks
for the coming of Jesus into the world.
We remember before you those who proclaim the Gospel
by living lives of holiness and goodness.
We pray for those preparing for Confirmation
and all who are seeking to know you better.

Silence

Let us praise the name of the Lord.
His name only is exalted.

We bring before you rulers of people,
politicians and leaders of nations.
We remember all who are striving
to bring peace and unity to humankind.
We think especially today of rescue workers,
of ambulance workers and firefighters.

Silence

Let us praise the name of the Lord.
His name only is exalted.

We give thanks that you care for us as our Father
and that we all belong to your family.
We pray for our own parents, families and friends.
May we know that you are with us and love us.

Silence

Let us praise the name of the Lord.
His name only is exalted.

You are our Redeemer and are with us in our troubles.
We remember all whose lives are endangered at this time,
all who are fearful and anxious.
We pray to you for those who are ill at home or in hospital.
We trust in your love and power.

Silence

Let us praise the name of the Lord.
His name only is exalted.

You save us from destruction
and have chosen us to be one with you in your kingdom.
We ask you to bless our loved ones departed
with your love and grace.

Silence

Merciful Father,
**accept these prayers
for the sake of your Son,
our Saviour Jesus Christ.
Amen.**

The Good Shepherd

Blessed are you, Lord our God.
When we were lost in our sin
you sent our Lord as the Good Shepherd to bring us home.
He descended into the depths to raise us to the heights;
he tasted death for us to know eternal life.
Blessed are you, Father, Son and Holy Spirit.

We give thanks for all who are called
to be shepherds of your people,
all who are guides and protectors.
We remember bishops and especially our bishop;
we pray for all priests and especially our own pastor.
Bless all who teach us the faith
and help us to walk in the way of holiness.

Silence

The Lord is my shepherd;
I shall fear no evil.

We ask you to give courage and strength
to all who work in the emergency services.
We pray for all ambulance crews and paramedics,
for air and sea rescue services
and for coastguards.
We remember the police and the fire crews.
Bless, O Lord, all who work
for the relief of poverty and suffering
among the poor of our world.

Silence

The Lord is my shepherd;
I shall fear no evil.

We give you thanks
for the safety and comfort of our homes.
We ask you to protect our loved ones
and guide them in the ways of peace.
Give wisdom and love to all who work
in the social services.
Comfort all who are lonely or feel unwanted.

Silence

The Lord is my shepherd;
I shall fear no evil.

God of love, we remember all
who have been involved in accidents this week.
We pray for all who have been injured
and those who are bereaved.
We pray for those who have gone into hospital
and all who are ill at home.

Silence

The Lord is my shepherd;
I shall fear no evil.

Good and gracious God,
you have rescued us from the darkness of death
and opened for us the way to eternal life.
We bring before you all our friends and loved ones
who are now with you in your kingdom.
Lord, grant them your love and light.

Silence

Merciful Father,
accept these prayers
for the sake of your Son,
our Saviour Jesus Christ.
Amen.

The Transfiguration

Blessed are you Lord God our Father.
You have revealed your hidden glory
in the face of our Lord Jesus Christ;
in Christ you have given us the hope of life eternal.
Bless your Church, O Lord,
with the radiance of your presence.
In each place of worship may we bow before your glory.
We ask you to transform with your brightness
all those places where worship
appears to be dull or lifeless.
Fill all preachers and teachers
with a vision of your glory.

Silence

Glorious God,
give us a glimpse of your glory.

Lord of light, transform the dark places of the world
by your presence.
We remember all who live in slums
and shanty towns,
all who live among war and dereliction.
Let the radiance of your presence
bring hope to their lives.

Silence

Glorious God,
give us a glimpse of your glory.

Glorious God, fill our homes with your love
and our lives with your glory.
Be with us and all our loved ones
and deliver us from darkness.

Silence

Glorious God,
give us a glimpse of your glory.

We remember all who suffer,
all who are in hospital,
all who are lonely and feel rejected,
all whose lives are in a dark cloud.
We think of those who are fearful of the future
and those whose lives are full of sadness.
Lord, may the light of your love transform their lives.

Silence

Glorious God,
give us a glimpse of your glory.

Give us a glimpse of your glory
and awareness of your gift of eternal life.
As we rejoice in the fellowship of all your saints,
grant to our loved ones departed
the joy and glory of your kingdom.

Silence

Merciful Father,
accept these prayers
for the sake of your Son,
our Saviour Jesus Christ.
Amen.

More than Possessions

Blessed are you, Lord God of all creation.
Through your goodness
we live in a rich and wonderful world.
You have given us the stewardship of your creation.
Lord, help us to work together
for the benefit of your whole world
and to reveal your glory within it.
May we strive for the protection and care
of all you have given into our charge.
Blessed are you, Father, Son and Holy Spirit.

God our Creator, we give you thanks
for the mystery of life and the beauty of the earth.
We remember in your presence
all who strive to reveal your glory.
We pray for churches throughout the world that seek
to help in the care and protection of the environment.
We ask your blessing on church groups
that work in areas of deprivation
and with people that are counted as of little importance.
We pray for all relief organisations
and those working with the world's poor.

Silence

Lord, in your love and goodness,
hear our prayer.

We give thanks for artists and craft workers,
for musicians and all who enrich our lives
by their talent and care.
We ask you to bless all who influence our future
by the decisions they make in governments
or in multinational companies.
We pray for the work of all who are involved
in conservation and in Fair Trade.

We remember the unemployed
and all who are denied human rights.
We ask your blessing
upon all oppressed and homeless people.

Silence

Lord, in your love and goodness,
hear our prayer.

We give thanks for our homes, our talents
and all that you have given to us.
May we use our resources for the benefit of those in need
and for the improvement of the world around us.
Bless our homes, that they may reflect your love
and be where your peace and your presence
are known to abide.

Silence

Lord, in your love and goodness,
hear our prayer.

Lord God, giver of life and health,
we come in our weakness to your strength,
in our troubles to your peace.
We ask your blessing upon all who are suffering,
all who are ill at home or in hospital.
We give thanks for the talent and attention of doctors,
nurses and all in the caring professions.
We pray especially for all who feel lonely or neglected
and all who have no one to care for them.

Silence

Lord, in your love and goodness,
hear our prayer.

Holy and merciful God, we rejoice in your saving power
and that you give us life that is eternal.
We ask your blessing upon all the saints
who have revealed your glory by their lives.
We remember also all who have enriched us
by their goodness and care,
and we pray for all our loved ones and friends
who are departed from us.

Silence

Merciful Father,
accept these prayers
for the sake of your Son,
our Saviour Jesus Christ.
Amen.

For or Against?

Blessed are you, Father, Son and Holy Spirit,
for you reveal your love to us
through our families and friends.
We learn of your care and protection
through the goodness and grace of our loved ones.
Teach us to learn to love as you love us.
Blessed are you, Father, Son and Holy Spirit.

We rejoice in the family of the Church.
May all who come find love and fellowship.
May they find acceptance and friendship.
Lord, help your Church be an instrument
of peace and healing in the world.
As we come together,
let us show the unity that is ours in Christ Jesus;
let us show one faith, one Church, one God.
We pray especially for unity among Christians,
that they may show a unity to the world.

Silence

Father, in your mercy,
hear your children's prayer.

We praise you, O God,
for the wonderful variety of people and talents
in the world.
We ask your blessing
on all areas of growth in goodness and grace.
We pray for schools, colleges and universities.
Lord, guide all who influence the minds of young people;
we pray for those who work with television
and in the pop-culture of today.

Silence

Father, in your mercy,
hear your children's prayer.

We give thanks
for all that enriches and encourages family life.

We pray for the social services
and all who support any families that are in difficulty.
We remember before you families
where there is great debt
or where love is absent.
Lord, bless our homes with your love and care.

Silence

Father, in your mercy,
hear your children's prayer.

We give thanks that you are a God who heals and restores,
that you care for our whole being –
body, mind and spirit.
We remember in your presence
all who have been injured in accidents
or through acts of violence,
all who have taken ill suddenly
and those whose illness has no cure.
We pray for their well-being
and the knowledge of your love.
Lord, bless all who share in healing.
We pray for our doctors and nurses
and all who work in hospitals.

Silence

Father, in your mercy,
hear your children's prayer.

Lord, in your power
all are restored and renewed in your heavenly kingdom.
We give thanks for all the saints
and we pray to you for our loved ones and friends
who are departed from us.

Silence

Merciful Father,
accept these prayers
for the sake of your Son,
our Saviour Jesus Christ.
Amen.

Master of Storms

Blessed are you, Lord our God,
for you are ever with us
and your presence brings us close to your power
and your peace.
You are ready to hear our cry
and to help us in our troubles.
We rejoice in your love and in your care.
Blessed are you, God, for ever,
Father, Son and Holy Spirit.

Almighty and loving God,
we seek to rest in your presence and in your peace.
The Church is often buffeted
by storms of antagonism and opposition.
We remember before you all Christians
who are struggling to survive in areas
where they face violence or ridicule for their faith.
We pray especially for those
whose lives are at risk at this time.
We remember also young Christians
who have to face opposition
from their friends and relatives.

Silence

Lord, in the storms of life we call upon you:
grant us your peace.

God our Creator, we rejoice in the well-being that is ours.
We remember in your presence
all who are suffering at this time
from storms, from floods, from drought.
We pray for all who are caught up in war,
in violence and acts of wickedness.
We remember all who are suffering from poverty
or who are in great debt.

Silence

Lord, in the storms of life we call upon you:
grant us your peace.

We give you thanks
for the love and protection of our homes.
Lord, grant that our loved ones may know your peace
and your presence.
We remember homes where people are not coping well,
where there are struggles in relationships.
We remember especially homes
where there are great tensions
between parents and their children.
Bless, O Lord, all whose homes have fallen apart
and all children who have been taken into care.

Silence

Lord, in the storms of life we call upon you:
grant us your peace.

God, you are ever-present.
We ask you to strengthen and support
all who are overwhelmed by the storms of life.
We remember those whose sickness finds no cure.
We pray for loved ones and carers who feel exhausted
and unable to cope any more.
Bless, O Lord, all who have been injured this week
or who have gone into hospital,
and all their loved ones who are anxious for them.

Silence

Lord, in the storms of life we call upon you:
grant us your peace.

Mighty God, when the last great storm overwhelms us
help us to know you are there
as the Lord and Giver of life;
to know we are not alone
and you will not let us perish.
Bless our loved ones who are departed
from the storms and troubles of this world
with your presence and your peace.

Silence

Merciful Father,
**accept these prayers
for the sake of your Son,
our Saviour Jesus Christ.
Amen.**

You Are the Christ

Blessed are you, Lord our God,
for you have sent your Son to be our Saviour.
In the darkness of this world he comes to be our light.
He has triumphed over pain and death
and opened to us the way to everlasting life.
He has revealed your love
and made us sons and daughters of God.
Blessed are you, Father, Son and Holy Spirit.

We give thanks for your saints
and for all who have stood against evil and temptation
in the world.
We remember before you all who at this time
are struggling with their faith,
all who are tempted away by false promises
and bright lights.
We pray for those who have learnt the words
but not met the Saviour.
We remember any who go through rituals
that seem empty of your presence.
Bless all who are being prepared for confirmation
and all who are seeking to grow
in their relationship with you.

Silence

O Lord, our Strength and our Redeemer,
hear our prayer.

We give thanks for the beauty of this day
and for the wonders of creation.
We remember before you all who are suffering
from war or division within communities.
We pray for those who have lost their way in life
and feel life has no meaning or purpose.
We ask your blessing upon all who strive
to improve our world and to create works of beauty.

Silence

O Lord, our Strength and our Redeemer,
hear our prayer.

We give thanks for the support of our families and friends,
for all the encouragement and help they give us.
We pray for homes where there is little encouragement
or where adventure and the fullness of life
are smothered by false securities.
We remember all who are homeless
and uncertain of their future.

Silence

O Lord, our Strength and our Redeemer,
hear our prayer.

We thank you for your love towards us.
We ask you to bless all who are struggling
with temptation and vice at this time.
We pray especially for any who live
in areas of degradation or evil.
We pray for all who struggle with weakness or illness,
especially those who cannot cope on their own.

Silence

O Lord, our Strength and our Redeemer,
hear our prayer.

We give thanks that through Christ
we are offered eternal life.
We remember the saints in glory
and our loved ones departed.
May they rejoice in your presence
and the fullness of life in your kingdom.

Silence

Merciful Father,
**accept these prayers
for the sake of your Son,
our Saviour Jesus Christ.
Amen.**

Death Bears Fruit

Blessed are you, Creator of life and joy.
We give you thanks for the promise of eternal life
offered through the death and resurrection
of your Son, Jesus Christ.
As we rejoice in the gift of this new day
we seek to delight in you and in your great love.
Blessed are you for ever.
We give thanks for all who have helped us
to grow in the faith,
for teachers and preachers, for shining examples,
for friends and relatives.
Bless all who seek to bring others to you,
all who by their goodness
show the world of your goodness.
We remember all who work in mission and outreach.

Silence

Holy and strong God,
help us to reveal your glory.

We give thanks for explorers and inventors,
for all who extend our experience
of the world and its mysteries.
We remember especially all who are involved in research.
We ask you to bless all who work in farming
and agriculture,
all who seek to provide us with food.
Help us to care for the hungry and the homeless.

Silence

Holy and strong God,
help us to reveal your glory.

We give thanks for those
who regularly sacrifice their time and energies for us.
We remember especially our parents
and all who care for us.
Lord, as we are loved, help us to show love to others.
We ask your blessing on all who feel unwanted or lonely.

Silence

Holy and strong God,
help us to reveal your glory.

We give you thanks for all medical research,
for the caring of doctors and nurses.
We pray for all who work in the emergency services
and those who risk their lives for others.
Lord, bless all who are ill, in pain or in danger
with an awareness of your love and care.

Silence

Holy and strong God,
help us to reveal your glory.

Glory be to you, O God,
for through our Saviour Jesus Christ
you have opened to us the way to eternal life.
We rejoice in the fellowship of all your saints.
We remember before you
our loved ones who are departed from us.

Silence

Merciful Father,
**accept these prayers
for the sake of your Son,
our Saviour Jesus Christ.
Amen.**

The Servant King

Blessed are you, Lord our God.
You have created us out of your love
and redeemed us by your love.
In the offering of our Lord Jesus on the cross
you have freed us from sin
and opened to us the way to eternal life.
Grant that, as Christ came not to be served but to serve,
we may give our lives in your service
and to the benefit of your world.
Blessed are you, Father, Son and Holy Spirit,
one God now and for ever.

Gracious God, you give us life and love.
Help us to give our life and love to you.
May the Church seek to serve the world
and to give itself for the benefit of the communities
in which it lives.
We ask you to bless all who are working
among the poor and the destitute.
We pray for prison visitors
and those who visit the ill and the lonely.
We remember all who reach out in love
to the outcasts and the neglected.
Bless the work of Christian Aid and all relief organisations.

Silence

Lord, our Saviour and Redeemer,
hear us and save us.

We give thanks for the caring professions
and for all who give their lives in the service of others.
We pray for doctors and nurses.
We remember the social services and care workers.
We ask your blessing upon all children who are in homes
or who are in need of protection.

We pray for the Children's Society
and all who work looking after children.

Silence

Lord, our Saviour and Redeemer,
hear us and save us.

Lord, we thank you for those
who have given us of themselves in love and care.
We pray for our parents and our families.
We ask you to bless all who have enriched us
by their goodness and their sacrifice for us.
Lord, teach us to be generous in our dealings
and sensitive to the needs of others.

Silence

Lord, our Saviour and Redeemer,
hear us and save us.

As we rejoice in your saving power,
we remember before you
all who work in the rescue services.
We pray for firefighters and ambulance workers,
for the lifeboat teams and the air and sea rescue crews.
We pray for all who have been involved in accidents
this week,
remembering the injured and the bereaved.
We ask your blessing upon all who are ill
at home or in hospital.

Silence

Lord, our Saviour and Redeemer,
hear us and save us.

Lord, we give thanks
that through the death and resurrection of Jesus
you have opened for us the way to life eternal.

We pray for all who have served you faithfully
here on earth
and are now in the fullness of your kingdom.
We remember our friends, benefactors and loved ones
who are departed from us:
may they be at peace with you.

Silence

Merciful Father,
accept these prayers
for the sake of your Son,
our Saviour Jesus Christ.
Amen.

Palm Sunday

Blessed are you, Lord God of all creation.
You have created us out of your love and for your love.
Help us to welcome you with songs of 'Hosanna',
knowing that you are our strength and our shield.
Help us to welcome Christ our Lord into our lives
as our Lord and Saviour.

Silence

I will give thanks to you, for you answered me,
and have become my salvation.

Lord, by you we are wonderfully created.
Help us to use our talents and lives
to the benefit of others and to your glory.
May your Church be an instrument of peace in the world.
Lord, forgive the divisions of your Church
and help us to see we are one in you.
Help us to work together to bring in your kingdom.

Silence

I will give thanks to you, for you answered me,
and have become my salvation.

Lord, we long for the time
when the kingdoms of the world
may become the kingdom of God.
Help us to work for peace and justice.
Bless the work of all who strive
to maintain and increase peace.
We pray especially for the United Nations.

Silence

I will give thanks to you, for you answered me,
and have become my salvation.

Lord, come and rule in our lives,
that there may be peace in our hearts and in our homes.
We remember before you
homes where there is conflict and violence,
where there is division and distress.

Silence

I will give thanks to you, for you answered me,
and have become my salvation.

God, we bring before you
the troubles and distress of peoples and nations.
We remember the hungry and homeless.
We ask you to bless
all who are not at peace with themselves,
all who are disturbed in mind or spirit.
We ask that all who are ill at this time
may know your love and your presence.

Silence

I will give thanks to you, for you answered me,
and have become my salvation.

We rejoice in the fellowship of all your saints.
We commend ourselves, our loved ones
and the faithful departed
to your love and your saving power.

Silence

Merciful Father,
accept these prayers
for the sake of your Son,
our Saviour Jesus Christ.
Amen.

EASTER
Easter Sunday

Blessed are you, God and Father of us all,
giver of life and life eternal.
By the love of your Son you have triumphed over hatred.
In his power, light has conquered darkness
and life has overcome death.
You have opened for us the gate of eternal life.
Blessed are you, O God, now and for ever.

Silence

Lord, we are Easter people:
let 'Alleluia' be our song.

We give you thanks and praise
for the resurrection of our Lord Jesus Christ
and for his appearances to his loved ones.
We rejoice with the whole Church
in the joy of the risen Lord.
May we who know the Good News
go and tell others that he is risen.
Grant that your Church may help to bring peace and hope
to a troubled world.
We ask you to give courage to all who have not seen
and yet believe.

Silence

Lord, we are Easter people:
let 'Alleluia' be our song.

Risen Lord, we seek your peace:
peace for our war-torn world;
peace between nations and people;
peace in our dealings with each other;
peace in our hearts and homes.

Silence

Lord, we are Easter people:
let 'Alleluia' be our song.

As you appeared to the disciples in the house,
come enter our homes;
come enter into our fear and darkness;
come enter into our enclosed lives and our fear to venture.
Come with the glorious freedom you offer
to the children of God.

Silence

Lord, we are Easter people:
let 'Alleluia' be our song.

We come with all who weep by gravesides,
all who mourn the loss of a loved one,
all who feel lonely or deserted.
May all who mourn find new hope and joy in you.
We remember all who are terminally ill
and those who are caring for them.
We think of those who have a heavy weight
on their hearts and minds
and tears in their eyes.
We ask that we may all know the hope of eternal life.

Silence

Lord, we are Easter people:
let 'Alleluia' be our song.

We rejoice with the disciples and all your saints
in the joy of the risen Lord.
We ask you to bless all our loved ones departed
with the fullness of your light and peace in eternal life.

Silence

Merciful Father,
accept these prayers
for the sake of your Son,
our Saviour Jesus Christ.
Amen.

Jesus Is Alive 1

Blessed are you, Lord God of our salvation.
To you be praise and glory for ever.
You have delivered us from the darkness of death
through your beloved Son.
In him, light has conquered darkness;
life has triumphed over death.
He has breathed into us your life-giving Spirit.
Blessed are you, Father, Son and Holy Spirit,
our God for ever and ever.

Lord, we give you thanks for the light of the Gospel
and that it shines in our hearts.
We rejoice in the resurrection and in your saving power.
We remember all who are struggling with their faith,
those who doubt,
any who sit in darkness or who live in fear.
We bring to mind all who have fallen away from the faith,
especially any known to us.

Silence

Lord God, you are light:
in you is no darkness at all.

We remember peoples and nations who feel drained
and lack energy.
We ask your blessing upon all who suffer
from poverty or oppression.
We pray for any who are separated
from their loved ones and their homes;
we remember all who are in prison.

Silence

Lord God, you are light:
in you is no darkness at all.

We give thanks
that you appeared in an ordinary home, O Christ.
We ask that your presence and your peace
may be known in our homes and among our loved ones.
We bring before you homes
where faith is mocked or persecuted,
and pray for all who are struggling to remain faithful.

Silence

Lord God, you are light:
in you is no darkness at all.

We think of all who are struggling with life:
homes where there is tension or lack of peace;
people who are ill and afraid of the future;
all who are lonely and facing a time of crisis.
May all know your presence and your peace.

Silence

Lord God, you are light:
in you is no darkness at all.

Father, we give you thanks
for the new life that you offer to us in your Son,
for you offer us eternal life.
We come to you with confidence
and pray for friends and loved ones departed.
May they know the fullness of joy in your presence
and in eternal life.

Silence

Merciful Father,
accept these prayers
for the sake of your Son,
our Saviour Jesus Christ.
Amen.

Jesus Is Alive 2

Blessed are you, mighty God,
Creator of light and darkness.
To you be praise and glory for ever.
By the resurrection of your Son to eternal life
you have destroyed the darkness and fear of death.
Radiant life is ours through him who loves us,
Jesus, our Lord and our friend.
Blessed are you, Father, Son and Holy Spirit,
our God for ever and ever.

We give thanks that you have called us
to witness to your resurrection and to your presence.
Help us, Lord Jesus, to turn away from sin
and to follow you.
May your Church reveal your glory to the world.
We remember today all who are persecuted for their faith,
all who are struggling to make your name known
in difficult areas.
We pray for all who are full of doubt or fear.

Silence

You set us free when we are hard-pressed.
Have mercy on us and hear our prayer.

We bring before you the fearful and the anxious;
all whose lives are in danger through violence or war.
We remember all who are locked away,
in prison or by painful memories,
all who are striving for new freedom and for hope.

Silence

You set us free when we are hard-pressed.
Have mercy on us and hear our prayer.

We give thanks for your presence in our homes:
that you are always with us.
May we know you as a friend and helper.
Bless our family and our loved ones
with your abiding presence.
Be known among our friends and our companions.
We remember all who live alone
and are worried about their lives or their future.

Silence

You set us free when we are hard-pressed.
Have mercy on us and hear our prayer.

We give thanks for the healing power of faith.
We ask you to bless and guide all who heal.
We remember our own doctor and surgery.
We ask that the ill and the weary may know you
as their companion and helper.
We pray to you for all who are hard-pressed
and struggling at this time,
especially for . . .

Silence

You set us free when we are hard-pressed.
Have mercy on us and hear our prayer.

Blessed are you, Lord Jesus Christ,
for you have triumphed over darkness and death,
opening for us the way to eternal life.
We remember in your presence
friends and loved ones who are departed from us.
May they rejoice in the fullness of life eternal.

Silence

Merciful Father,
accept these prayers
for the sake of your Son,
our Saviour Jesus Christ.
Amen.

JESUS AND HIS PEOPLE
The Vine

Blessed are you, Lord our God,
for you have created us out of your love
and for your love.
We know that we abide in you and that you are in us
by the Spirit that you have given us.
As you love us, help us to love one another,
Father, Son and Holy Spirit.

Lord, bless the Church with the knowledge
of your indwelling presence.
May we learn to abide in you and know that you are in us.
Give wisdom to all who go out in mission
and all who preach your word.
We pray for the young in the faith,
that they will be given the opportunity
to grow and bear fruit.
We remember all study groups, Bible classes
and Sunday schools.

Silence

Lord, you abide in us;
we ask that we may abide in you.

We remember the nations of the world
and especially those who are not at peace at this time.
We ask your guidance on all who care
for the world's poor, refugees and war-torn peoples.
We pray for the time when the kingdoms of this world
may become the kingdom of Christ our Lord.

Silence

Lord, you abide in us;
we ask that we may abide in you.

We give thanks for all who have shared their faith with us.
In our turn may we also bear fruit
and bring others to the love and presence of our God.
Lord, bless our homes with the glory of your presence.
Help us to live in and share your peace.

Silence

Lord, you abide in us;
we ask that we may abide in you.

We bring before you all who doubt or despair,
all who are surrounded by darkness or illness.
May they come into the light of your love
and know that you are with them.
We ask you to bless all who have been involved
in accidents or in violence this week.
Give courage and hope to all
who seek to bring your healing and peace.

Silence

Lord, you abide in us;
we ask that we may abide in you.

Lord, you abide with us through life
and we abide with you through death.
In your love you have given us eternal life
through Christ our risen Lord.
We give you thanks for this great gift.
We ask that you bless all our loved ones departed
with the joy of your love and your presence.

Silence

Merciful Father,
accept these prayers
for the sake of your Son,
our Saviour Jesus Christ.
Amen.

Friends

Blessed are you, Lord God, who through your Son
has revealed your great love for us
and in his resurrection gave us a Friend and a Saviour.
We rejoice in your presence this day
with the joy and the freedom of the children of God.
Blessed are you, our God for ever.

As you have called us to be friends,
to reveal your love and the joy of your presence,
we come with sorrow for the divisions
of the Church and the world.
We seek forgiveness for rivalry and disunity
within the Church.
Lord, strengthen us in love
and lead us to a unity that reflects that we are one in you.
May any divisions within our community be healed
and well-being restored.

Silence

Lord, as you love us,
help us to love one another.

We come before you as part of a world
caught up in violence, war, hatred, greed and hunger.
There are people who are oppressed and treated as slaves.
There are people who are counted as nothing,
rejected and unloved.
Lord, forgive us and change us.
Strengthen all who work
for the peace and well-being of all.
May we share in the care of all suffering people.

Silence

Lord, as you love us,
help us to love one another.

We give you thanks for all our loved ones,
for their generosity and sacrifice for us.
We remember all who feel unloved and unwanted.
We pray for homes where there is hatred or violence,
where there is little respect for each other,
where there is neglect.
We ask your blessing upon all
who have been taken into care.

Silence

Lord, as you love us,
help us to love one another.

Lord of love, we remember before you all who are lonely.
We ask your blessing upon those who are ill or injured.
We pray for all who are raging against life
and all who are not at peace with themselves
or the world.
We pray for all who have hardened their hearts
against love.

Silence

Lord, as you love us,
help us to love one another.

We rejoice in your saving love
and that you have called us to eternal life.
We remember loved ones departed from us.
As we give thanks for their friendship
we pray that they may know you as their friend
in your eternal kingdom.

Silence

Merciful Father,
accept these prayers
for the sake of your Son,
our Saviour Jesus Christ.
Amen.

One Church

Blessed are you, Lord our God,
for you welcome us whenever we turn to you:
you are always ready to hear us and to help us.
We rejoice in your presence
and ask that we may show your love
and your saving power in the world.
Blessed are you, Father, Son and Holy Spirit.

We give thanks for your Church throughout the world.
May the Church be an instrument
of peace and reconciliation
between peoples and nations.
Bless the churches within our area:
may we learn to work together in unity
and in witness to your saving power.
We pray for churches that are struggling to survive
and that are in areas of hostility or apathy.

Silence

Lord, our strength and our redeemer,
hear our prayer.

Father, we give thanks for the peace that you offer us.
We remember in your presence
all who are living in areas of war and violence.
We pray for those who suffer attacks on their communities,
for those who are victims of ethnic cleansing or genocide.
We ask your blessing upon all communities
whose way of life and livelihood are threatened.

Silence

Lord, our strength and our redeemer,
hear our prayer.

Father, we thank you for all our loved ones and friends,
for those who have enriched our lives
through their goodness and example.
We ask you to bless and protect them.
We pray for homes where relationships are breaking down,
especially where there is violence or neglect.
We pray for all who are suffering
through losing a loved one.

Silence

Lord, our strength and our redeemer,
hear our prayer.

Father, we bring to your love
the suffering and sorrow of our world.
We remember in your presence all who are ill
at home or in hospital.
We pray for those involved in accidents
or acts of cruelty and violence this week.
We bring before you all who live in fear
and those who feel they can no longer cope with life.

Silence

Lord, our strength and our redeemer,
hear our prayer.

Father, you created us for yourself and for your love.
As we give our love to you,
we pray for all our loved ones who are departed from us.
May they rejoice in the light of your presence
and in the fullness of eternal life.

Silence

Merciful Father,
**accept these prayers
for the sake of your Son,
our Saviour Jesus Christ.
Amen.**

ASCENSION
Choosing an Apostle

Blessed are you, Lord our God.
You are always with us and ready to hear our prayers.
You have called us by our name
and wait for us to turn to you.
You have chosen us to work with you
and you seek to fill us with your Spirit.
Blessed are you, Father, Son and Holy Spirit.

We give you thanks for men and women of prayer
who have revealed your love
and helped us to know of your presence.
We remember before you
all who are evangelists and ministers,
all who proclaim your love for us.
May we share in the ministry and the outreach
of your Church.

Silence

Lord, as we wait upon you,
hear our prayer.

We bring before you the troubles and the sadness
of our world.
We pray for all who have lost their vision,
who are blind to goodness
and unaware of your presence or your love.
We remember especially
all who feel that life is without purpose and meaningless.

Silence

Lord, as we wait upon you,
hear our prayer.

We thank you for all who love us,
for our families and our friends.
We know that you reveal your love through their love.
We ask your blessing on homes where there is little love
or where there is violence and neglect.
May we welcome you into our homes
and into our friendships.

Silence

Lord, as we wait upon you,
hear our prayer.

We give thanks to all who have been called
to share in your healing powers.
Bless all doctors and nurses,
all who work in hospitals or are part of ambulance crews.
We remember before you all who are struggling with life,
those who are ill or lonely, anxious or depressed.

Silence

Lord, as we wait upon you,
hear our prayer.

We rejoice that our Lord shares in our prayers
and makes intercession for us in heaven.
We pray for all our loved ones who have died
and are now in your keeping.

Silence

Merciful Father,
accept these prayers
for the sake of your Son,
our Saviour Jesus Christ.
Amen.

PENTECOST
The Power of the Spirit

Blessed are you, Lord our God.
Your Spirit comes to our weakness with his power.
In the strength of your Spirit
you enable us to live and work to your praise and glory.
May we who have received the gifts of the Spirit
use them for the benefit of your creation
and to reveal your love in the world.
Blessed are you, Lord God, Father, Son and Holy Spirit.

Lord, as we rejoice in the coming of the Spirit
we give thanks for all who proclaim your presence
and power.
We remember all preachers and evangelists,
all who celebrate the sacraments and minister to us.
May all your people share fully
in forwarding the Gospel and revealing your love.

Silence

We rejoice that you fill our world.
Your Spirit is with us.

Lord, you give great gifts and talents to your people.
We ask you to bless and guide all leaders
of nations and peoples,
all who make decisions that will affect our lives
and the future of the world.
We pray for scientists and research workers,
for all who work in providing us with news
or influence us through the press and television.

Silence

We rejoice that you fill our world.
Your Spirit is with us.

We give thanks that your Holy Spirit
came upon the disciples in an ordinary home.
Bless our homes with your presence
and grant that there we may grow in the fruits of the Spirit.
Let us know you are with our loved ones and us.
Protect us from all evil
and guide us by your Spirit
in the ways of peace and love.

Silence

We rejoice that you fill our world.
Your Spirit is with us.

Lord of life, we remember all who are dis-spirited,
the distressed, the depressed and despairing,
all who have lost hope or joy in their lives.
We pray for all who fear the future,
all who have lost sight of you and your love.
We remember also all who are struggling
with poverty or hunger,
the homeless and the refugee.
We pray for all who are ill.

Silence

We rejoice that you fill our world.
Your Spirit is with us.

We give you praise, Lord, giver of life and life eternal.
We rejoice that you renew, refresh and restore us.
We remember in your presence
your blessed saints and our loved ones departed;
may light perpetual shine upon them
as they share in the glory of your kingdom.

Silence

Merciful Father,
accept these prayers
for the sake of your Son,
our Saviour Jesus Christ.
Amen.

TRINITY
A Balanced Idea of God

Blessed are you, Lord God, Father of all creation.
To you be praise and glory for ever.
Your Son Jesus Christ brings light
to dispel our darkness and hope to banish our fears.
He sends upon us your promised Spirit
to strengthen and guide us.
Through your great grace and goodness
help us to reveal your love in all the world.
Blessed are you, Father, Son and Holy Spirit.

Father, we give thanks
for the wonders and mystery of creation.
We thank you for life and for your love.
We ask you to bless the nations of the world
as they strive for unity and peace.
We remember all who work in caring for our planet,
all who work in conservation
and in growing our food.

Silence

Holy, holy, holy God,
hear us and help us.

Jesus, you are our Redeemer.
You gave yourself in love for us.
We come to give our love to you.
We remember in your presence
all who lack any knowledge of love.
We pray for all who are scorned and rejected,
especially those who suffer
from the cruelty and wickedness of others.
We ask you to bless all who are struggling at this time.

Silence

Holy, holy, holy God,
hear us and help us.

Holy Spirit, inspirer and giver of talents,
we thank you for artists and crafts people,
for all who beautify and enrich our earth.
We remember in your presence
all who are unable to use their talents
because of the situation in which they live.
We remember those who are restricted
by poverty or tyranny.

Silence

Holy, holy, holy God,
hear us and help us.

Holy and blessed Trinity, Three Persons and One God,
we thank you for your love which is eternal.
We thank you for the gift of personality.
We remember in your presence
friends and loved ones who are departed from us.
May they rejoice in the fullness of life eternal
in your presence and in your kingdom.

Silence

Merciful Father,
accept these prayers
for the sake of your Son,
our Saviour Jesus Christ.
Amen.

JESUS HEALS 1
Healing and Prayer

Blessed are you, Lord God Almighty.
You are the giver of life and power;
all energy, all strength comes from you.
We come to you for renewal and refreshment.
We come to rest in your presence
that we may find strength and hope in you.

We pray for all who preach the word
and administer the sacraments,
that they may find great strength from your presence.
May the Church be a place of stillness and refreshment.
May your people show
that you give joy and peace to their lives.

Silence

Lord God, we wait before you.
Renew our strength.

We pray for all who are responsible
for the limited resources of our world,
that we may use them with respect and care.
We ask your blessing
on all who provide our homes with power and light:
those who work in the oil, gas and electric industries.
We remember all who are in emerging nations
and are looking to new sources of power.

Silence

Lord God, we wait before you.
Renew our strength.

We pray for all who expend their energies
in caring for us and loving us.
We ask you to bless our homes and our loved ones.
We pray for those who have taught us
and all who have provided for our needs.

Silence

Lord God, we wait before you.
Renew our strength.

Father, all-powerful,
we remember the needs of the weary,
the powerless, the ill.
We ask your blessing on all who feel
that they cannot cope with life
or who are drained of their resources.
We pray especially for those who are terminally ill.

Silence

Lord God, we wait before you.
Renew our strength.

Father, you are the giver of life and life eternal.
We remember in your presence
the holy ones who have served you.
We pray for our loved ones departed,
that all may be renewed by your power.

Silence

Merciful Father,
accept these prayers
for the sake of your Son,
our Saviour Jesus Christ.
Amen.

Healing and Forgiveness

Blessed are you, Lord our God.
You forgive us our sins and cleanse us from all iniquity.
You give us the chance to start every day anew.

Lord, may your Church be an accepting and loving Church.
May it help to free those who are paralysed
by fear and doubt.
May it reach out to those who do not know of your love
and bring them to you.
We remember we are part of your mission
and we pray for all who are involved in outreach.

Silence

Holy and strong one,
let us rejoice in your saving power.

We remember in your presence
all who are struggling to survive.
We pray for those suffering from drought or flood,
all who are underfed or homeless.
Bless all who work for the relief of the poor and troubled.
We remember the work of Christian Aid, the Red Cross
and all who are good neighbours.

Silence

Holy and strong one,
let us rejoice in your saving power.

We give you thanks for our friends and family,
especially for those who brought us to know you.
We pray for all who teach in our church
and all who set an example of care and love
in our community.

Silence

Holy and strong one,
let us rejoice in your saving power.

Lord, let your presence bring comfort to the suffering;
may they know your love and care.
We remember all who are paralysed
or suffering from strokes,
all who are unable to move about freely
and all who are housebound.

Silence

Holy and strong one,
let us rejoice in your saving power.

We give thanks for the power of the Resurrection,
and that you offer us life eternal.
We remember all who have lost loved ones this week
and we pray for our loved ones departed.

Silence

Merciful Father,
**accept these prayers
for the sake of your Son,
our Saviour Jesus Christ.
Amen.**

The Authority of Jesus

Gracious God,
you give us a glimpse of your glory
in the face of Jesus Christ.
Through him we are able to come before your presence
and to rejoice in your love.
Through him alone
we are counted worthy to approach you.
We give you thanks and praise
for the coming of Jesus into our world.

Silence

Lord of all power and might,
hear our prayer.

We remember in your presence
all who have not heard the Good News.
We pray for those
who do not know anything of being healed or forgiven.
Grant that the Church may proclaim
your love and saving power.
We pray for all who administer the sacraments
and who preach the word.

Silence

Lord of all power and might,
hear our prayer.

We pray for areas of our world
where darkness seems to triumph over light.
We remember people who are possessed by drug addiction.
We remember also those
who feel that they are possessed by evil.
May they all come to know the glorious liberty
of the children of God.

Silence

Lord of all power and might,
hear our prayer.

We give you thanks and praise
for those who have shared their faith with us,
for all who have encouraged us in the way of goodness.
We ask your blessing upon them
and upon our loved ones and friends.

Silence

Lord of all power and might,
hear our prayer.

We pray for all who have been ill for a long time,
for those whose illness finds no cure.
We pray for all
who feel they are losing their faculties or mobility,
all who cannot cope on their own.
We remember those who are in hospices.

Silence

Lord of all power and might,
hear our prayer.

We rejoice in the fellowship of the saints.
We remember loved ones who are departed from us.
We commend the whole of creation and ourselves
to your unfailing love.

Silence

Merciful Father,
accept these prayers
for the sake of your Son,
our Saviour Jesus Christ.
Amen.

Against the Rules?

Blessed are you, Lord our God,
for you have created light to dispel the darkness
and have shone in our hearts
to give the light of the knowledge of the glory of God
in the face of Jesus Christ.
We rejoice that all power and might come from you.
Blessed be God for ever.

Loving God, we pray for all who do not know or love you.
We remember especially
those who have hardened their hearts against you.
We pray for all whose life is joyless
or governed by rules rather than love.
May your Church be willing to accept and welcome
all who come seeking you and your love.
Teach us to be generous in our dealings with each other.

Silence

Lord, bringing light out of darkness,
let us share in your love.

We give thanks for the many talents and abilities
of your people.
We rejoice in each other's gifts and uniqueness.
We pray for all who are restricted
by tyranny or the dominance of others.
We remember all who are in refugee camps
or are homeless.
We pray for all who feel unloved and neglected.

Silence

Lord, bringing light out of darkness,
let us share in your love.

We thank you for our homes
and the love and acceptance that is there.
We pray for homes where life is oppressive
or adventure smothered.

We remember all who are leaving home for the first time
and all their loved ones.
We give you thanks for homes
where there are new members of the family
and where all are growing in love.

Silence

Lord, bringing light out of darkness,
let us share in your love.

Loving God, we pray for all who walk in darkness
and live in fear.
We think especially of those who are persecuted,
abused or neglected.
We remember before you
all who are depressed and lonely,
all who are struggling to survive.
We remember also all who are ill
and all who have been injured in accidents
or acts of violence.
We think especially of those who are now disabled
or restricted by illness.

Silence

Lord, bringing light out of darkness,
let us share in your love.

Lord of life, we rejoice
that you have destroyed the darkness of death
and opened for us the way to eternal life.
In love we bring before you our dear ones departed,
praying they may rejoice in your light.
In fellowship with all the saints,
we offer you our love and ourselves.

Silence

Merciful Father,
**accept these prayers
for the sake of your Son,
our Saviour Jesus Christ.
Amen.**

FOLLOWING JESUS
Called

Blessed are you, Lord our God,
for you have called us out of darkness
into your most glorious light.
In calling us, you give our lives direction and purpose:
you offer us the opportunity
to reveal your love and your presence to the world.
Blessed are you, Father, Son and Holy Spirit,
one God now and for ever.

Lord, we give thanks that you have called us
to know you and love you.
Keep our ears open to your call
and our hearts open to your love.
Bless, O Lord, each in their vocation,
that every life may be filled
with purpose and meaning through you.
We remember all who have never heard or known you,
all who feel that life is empty or without purpose.
We ask you to guide all who preach
and teach of your presence.
We pray for all who feel thwarted in their vocations
by circumstance or illness;
may they know that God still calls them where they are.
We pray for the Mission to Seafarers
and all who care for those who work on the sea.

Silence

Lord you have called us:
help us to fulfil our calling.

We give thanks for all who are called
to govern and guide the nations of the world.

We ask your blessing on Elizabeth our queen
and on all in authority.
We pray for all who are called
to bring peace and maintain peace throughout the world,
especially any who are risking their lives for others.
We pray for the work of the United Nations.
We remember before you all who work upon the sea,
fishermen and merchant seamen,
all who are crewing lifeboats and who are coastguards.

Silence

Lord you have called us:
help us to fulfil our calling.

We give thanks for those who have taught us
of you and your love,
for those who have guided us in awareness of you.
We ask your blessing upon our homes,
our families and friends.
May we reveal your glory in our lives.
We remember all who are called to be parents
and ask your blessing upon them and their children.
We pray for any who feel unable to cope
with their families or with relationships.

Silence

Lord you have called us:
help us to fulfil our calling.

Holy and strong One, we remember before you
all who suffer from weakness or illness,
all who suffer from being handicapped
or restricted in their lives.
May they know that you love them
and continue to call them.
We ask your blessing on all who are called to work
in hospitals, surgeries and health centres.
We pray for friends and loved ones who are ill.

Silence

Lord you have called us:
help us to fulfil our calling.

Lord, you call us to yourself and to life eternal.
May we learn to enjoy you and our calling
this day and for ever.
We rejoice in the fellowship of all your saints.
We pray for our friends and loved ones
who are departed from us.
May we with them have a share in your eternal kingdom.

Silence

Merciful Father,
**accept these prayers
for the sake of your Son,
our Saviour Jesus Christ.
Amen.**

Different Responses

Blessed are you, Lord God, giver of life and light.
You give us of your love:
you give us of yourself.
Open our ears to your call and our hearts to your love.
Send us out in the power of your Spirit
to proclaim the Good News of your saving love
as revealed in our Saviour Jesus Christ.
Blessed are you, Father, Son and Holy Spirit.

We give thanks that you sent Jesus to live among us.
We pray that we may share in his mission,
that we may pass on the message of the Gospel
and show acts of mercy that reveal God's love.
May your whole Church be moved to share
in the ministry that is theirs.
We remember today all involved in the healing ministry.
We ask you to bless all counsellors, spiritual directors
and all who lead us in our ministry.

Silence

Lord, hear us:
show us your loving kindness.

We remember all who are suffering
under totalitarian states,
all who are oppressed
and forced to do what they do not want to do.
We ask your blessing on all who are seeking
to bring liberty and freedom to captive peoples.
Give courage and strength
to all who are working for relief agencies
and generosity to all who are called upon
to support them in their work.

Silence

Lord, hear us:
show us your loving kindness.

We give thanks for our homes and loved ones.
Through our families teach us to be sensitive
to the needs of others;
help us to listen carefully and to respond quickly.
We ask your blessing upon all
who have stopped communicating properly
with each other,
that they may again be awakened
to those with whom they live and work.

Silence

Lord, hear us:
show us your loving kindness.

We give thanks that you, O God, care for us,
body, mind and spirit.
We remember in your presence all suffering people.
We pray especially for those who feel no one listens
or cares.
We ask you to bless all who are homeless,
all who are deeply in debt.
We pray for all who are drug addicts
and all who cannot cope with life.
We remember all who are ill in our own community.

Silence

Lord, hear us:
show us your loving kindness.

We rejoice in the Good News of eternal life.
We remember in your presence
friends and loved ones who are departed from us.
We share with them in the fellowship of all your saints
and commend them and ourselves to your unfailing love.

Silence

Merciful Father,
**accept these prayers
for the sake of your Son,
our Saviour Jesus Christ.
Amen.**

Faithfulness

Blessed are you, Lord God.
You have called us into life,
to love and serve you.
You have promised that you are with us always
and that you are our Helper and our Guide.

We give thanks for all who hear and obey your call:
for men and women who willingly sacrifice
and deprive themselves
for the good of others.
We remember all who have spent their lives
in your service.
We ask you to give strength to all who are quietly seeking
to give you their love and their lives.
We remember today all who suffer rejection,
pain or distress
for following you.

Silence

Lord, as you have called us,
hear us when we call upon you.

We remember with gratitude
all who have given their lives in research and exploration
for the good of others.
We ask you to bless all scientists, technicians
and leaders of people.
We pray for those working among the poor
and the deprived of our world.

Silence

Lord, as you have called us,
hear us when we call upon you.

We give thanks for all our parents and loved ones do for us,
for their love, their sacrifice and their care.
We seek your blessing upon our homes and our families.
We remember all who have no one to care for them.

Silence

Lord, as you have called us,
hear us when we call upon you.

We give thanks for the dedication of doctors
and nurses and hospital staff.
We ask your blessing on all who are in hospital
or who are ill at this time
and upon all who look after them.
We remember all who feel that no one cares about them.

Silence

Lord, as you have called us,
hear us when we call upon you.

We rejoice that you have called us to eternal life
and that you have invited us
to enjoy your presence for ever.
We pray for all who have given their lives
in the service of others,
and for our loved ones departed.
May they now rejoice in the fullness of your kingdom.

Silence

Merciful Father,
**accept these prayers
for the sake of your Son,
our Saviour Jesus Christ.
Amen.**

JESUS HEALS 2
Only Believe

Blessed are you, O God,
our Lord, King of the Universe, God of our fathers,
our Creator, Redeemer, Sustainer.
From you come life, renewal and refreshment.
In you we find hope, restoration and well-being.
We believe in you, we trust you.
Blessed are you, Father, Son and Holy Spirit.

We give thanks for the Church throughout the world;
for people who are growing in the faith
and being made strong by their beliefs.
We remember all who are struggling
with opposition and evil
and all whose lives are in danger.
We remember all who feel oppressed and let down.
We pray for all whose faith is being challenged
and those who have lost contact with you.

Silence

Lord, through contact with you
help us to rise.

Lord, we rejoice in the lives and talents
of the people of our world.
We pray to you for all whose gifts are being wasted
through poor education or through tyranny.
We remember all whose ambitions and livelihood
have been destroyed through war or natural disasters.
We ask your blessing upon all who
are counted as untouchable or are rejected by society.

Silence

Lord, through contact with you
help us to rise.

We give you praise and thanks for all who care for us.
We ask your blessing upon our families and friends,
all whom we love and all who love us.
We remember homes were there is serious illness
and where loved ones are carers.
We pray especially for all who are struggling
to keep their homes together,
all whose physical or financial resources are running out.

Silence

Lord, through contact with you
help us to rise.

We give thanks for all healers,
for doctors and nurses, for social workers and carers.
We remember all who are strengthened
by their faith and trust in you.
We ask you to bless all whose sickness finds no cure.
We pray for the terminally ill
and all who are in a hospice
or need permanent care in a home.
We pray for all who feel their life is wasting away.

Silence

Lord, through contact with you
help us to rise.

Lord, you are the giver of life and life eternal.
We rejoice in your presence and in your love.
We give you thanks for the resurrection
and the hope of eternal life.
We remember in your presence
our friends and loved ones who are departed from us.

We rejoice in the fellowship of all your saints.
We commend the whole world and ourselves
to your unfailing love.

Silence

Merciful Father,
accept these prayers
for the sake of your Son,
our Saviour Jesus Christ.
Amen.

Open to All

Blessed are you, Lord our God,
for you have called your people
from every tribe, nation and language.
We rejoice that you care for all peoples
and every single individual
and seek to offer each of them your love.
You have called us all to hear your word
and to proclaim your praises.
Blessed are you, Father, Son and Holy Spirit.

We rejoice that your Church is for all people
in all times and in all places.
No one who comes to you is cast out.
May we seek to make your Church
open and welcoming to all.
We ask your blessing upon all who are involved
in the outreach and mission of the church.
We remember especially those who seek
to proclaim your love by word and example.
We pray for all who have not heard of you
and your saving grace.

Silence

God, ever with us,
be our strength and our Saviour.

We give thanks for the peace
that you offer to us and to the nations.
We remember before you areas where there is conflict
and violence,
where people are caught up in war.
We pray for all who suffer from racial hatred
or prejudice,
all who are outcasts or refugees.
We ask your blessing upon the work of the United Nations
and all peacekeeping forces.

Silence

God, ever with us,
be our strength and our Saviour.

We give thanks for those who brought us
to know you and your love.
We pray for all who have taught us and cared for us.
We ask your blessing upon our families and our friends.
We remember before you all who are lonely
or feel uncared for and unwanted.

Silence

God, ever with us,
be our strength and our Saviour.

We give thanks for the gifts of hearing and speech.
We remember all who suffer from deafness
and those who are unable to speak.
We pray for all who suffer from autism,
all who are withdrawn from normal life
and all who find communication difficult.
We ask your blessing upon all ill and suffering people.
We remember especially
friends and members of our community who are ill.

Silence

God, ever with us,
be our strength and our Saviour.

We rejoice that you have opened for us
the fullness of eternal life and the way to your kingdom.
We remember friends and loved ones
who are departed from us.
May they enjoy knowing you in glory
and rest in the peace of your presence.

Silence

Merciful Father,
accept these prayers
for the sake of your Son,
our Saviour Jesus Christ.
Amen.

Jesus Opens Our Eyes

Blessed are you, Lord God.
You created light out of darkness
and gave us eyes to see the beauty and wonders
of your creation.
Lord, through the visible things of this world
lead us to see the invisible;
extend our vision beyond our eyes
that we may see with our hearts also.
Blessed are you, Father, Son and Holy Spirit.

We give thanks for the beauty and colour of our world,
for the gift of sight.
We ask your blessing upon men and women
who help us to see beyond the obvious,
upon all who are prophets and visionaries.
We pray for all who study your word
and who celebrate your sacraments.
We remember those training for ministry
and ask your blessing upon theological colleges
and all who teach Religious Education.

Silence

Lord, open our eyes
to see the invisible.

We give thanks for explorers, discoverers and inventors;
for all who have enriched the world by their wisdom
or by extending themselves.
We ask your blessing upon the leaders of nations,
upon governments and ruling bodies.
We pray for the United Nations
and all peacekeeping forces.
We remember today all writers and broadcasters,
artists and craft workers,
and all who influence our lives by their actions.

Silence

Lord, open our eyes
to see the invisible.

We rejoice in the protection and the peace of our homes.
We thank you for our families and friends
and ask your blessing upon them.
We pray for families who have become bored with life
and with each other,
for couples who have lost the spirit of exploration
and adventure.
We ask your blessing upon all who influence
the minds of the young and the vulnerable.

Silence

Lord, open our eyes
to see the invisible.

Lord we give thanks for all who have guided us
into the ways of goodness and love,
all who have enriched our lives by their wisdom.
We remember before you
all who have lost their way in life.
We pray for the confused, the disillusioned
and the despairing.
We remember all who are ill at home or in hospital.
We pray especially for all who suffer from blindness
or partial vision.

Silence

Lord, open our eyes
to see the invisible.

Lord, open our eyes to your kingdom
that is growing among us;
let us see your presence and love at work.
We give thanks for your saints
and for all our loved ones who have departed this life.

May they rejoice where faith has vanished into sight
in the glory of eternal life.

Silence

Merciful Father,
accept these prayers
for the sake of your Son,
our Saviour Jesus Christ.
Amen.

GOD'S WORLD AND ITS KING
Love and Respect

Blessed are you, Lord our God,
for you have created the world and all that is in it
out of your love and for your love.
You offer us a relationship with you
through your creation and through each other.
Teach us to care for your world and to respect all peoples.
Blessed are you, Father, Son and Holy Spirit.

We give you thanks and praise for the beauty of the earth
and the wonders of each creature.
Lord, help us to have a reverence and awe
for all that you have made.
May your Church encourage a sense of wonder
in all our dealings.
We remember the Church working among
oppressed peoples
and all who are treated as unimportant or dispensable.
Let us all learn good stewardship
of the gifts and the world you have given to us.

Silence

God our Creator,
in your love, hear us.

We praise you for the diversity of life on our planet,
for the balance of nature and the goodness of the earth.
We ask your blessing on areas and creatures
that are endangered.
We pray for the people of the rain forests
and for primitive tribes that are being robbed of their land.

Lord, guide the decisions of all who influence
the future of the earth.
We pray for multinational companies
and for all who wield power.

Silence

God our Creator,
in your love, hear us.

We give you thanks
for all who have shown us love and care.
We remember before you our families and friends
and all our loved ones.
We ask your blessing on all who feel lonely,
all who are neglected
and all whose relationships are breaking down.
We pray for any who have lost a loved one this week
or who have been deserted by a loved one.

Silence

God our Creator,
in your love, hear us.

As we rejoice in life
we pray for all who are doing genetic research
and all who probe into the mystery of life.
May your blessing be upon all who make discoveries
that deeply influence our lives.
We remember all who are struggling.
We pray for those who have lost any sense of wonder or joy,
the depressed and the disillusioned.
Lord, comfort all who are ill
and all who are finding life difficult.

Silence

God our Creator,
in your love, hear us.

We give thanks for the mystery of our own life
and that you are with us always.
We ask your blessing on all who have departed from us
and pray that they may rejoice
in the glory of your presence in your kingdom.

Silence

Merciful Father,
**accept these prayers
for the sake of your Son,
our Saviour Jesus Christ.
Amen.**

The Kingship of Christ

Blessed are you, Lord our God, King of the Universe.
All things are in your control and in your power
for you are almighty.
In the troubles and darkness of our world
help us to know your presence and your love.
May we know that though we are beset by many troubles
we cannot for a moment fall out of the everlasting arms
and that we are on our way to everlasting life
in the fullness of your kingdom.
Blessed are you, almighty and ever loving God,
Father, Son and Holy Spirit.

We rejoice this day that Jesus is the King of kings
and Lord of lords.
We give thanks that through him
we have the victory and triumph
over all that would seek to defeat us.
We pray that your Church may walk with confidence,
trusting in you and your love.
May we reveal your loving care
for the whole of your creation.
We remember Christians who are struggling
to bring peace and love to areas of hatred and strife.
Lord, may each of us seek to do your will.

Silence

Lord, your kingdom come.
Your will be done.

We look forward to the time
when the kingdoms of the world
will become the kingdom of Christ the King.
We remember this day all who are suffering
from tyranny or despotic rulers,
all who suffer through famine or flood.

We pray for any who feel that life is beyond their control
and all who feel utterly helpless.
Lord, bless all who strive to bring freedom and prosperity
to the peoples of the world.

Silence

Lord, your kingdom come.
Your will be done.

We give thanks that you are our guide and helper
in all of life.
We ask your blessing on our homes and our loved ones.
May your kingdom be revealed and your will be done
in all that we do and say.
We pray for families who are suffering at this time
from debt and poverty,
from difficulties in relationships and
from watching a loved one who is ill.

Silence

Lord, your kingdom come.
Your will be done.

We rejoice, O Lord, in your saving power.
We remember before you all who are ill
at home or in hospital,
all who struggle to survive
and all who are oppressed in any way.
We ask your blessing upon all who will find this
a difficult week,
those who will have to face hard decisions
and those who feel they have little or no freedom.

Silence

Lord, your kingdom come.
Your will be done.

We put our trust in you, O God,
and in the promise of the fullness of your kingdom.
We remember before you
all who have departed from this world
and are now at peace with you.
We pray for loved ones and friends who have died.
We rejoice in the fellowship of all the saints
and pray that we may share with them
in your eternal kingdom.

Silence

Merciful Father,
accept these prayers
for the sake of your Son,
our Saviour Jesus Christ.
Amen.